The Well: New and S

MW00966076

The Well: New and Selected Poems

Kenneth Sherman

For Sydney

All good things,

Kenneth
Sherman /08

Wolsak and Wynn . Toronto

Typeset in Garamond, printed in Canada by
The Coach House Printing Company, Toronto.

Front cover art: Marie Sherman
Cover design: The Coach House Printing Company
Author's photograph: Justine Sherman

The author is grateful to the editors of the following journals where some of the new poems have appeared or are about to appear: *Descant, The Fiddlehead, The Malahat Review, The New Quarterly, Parchment*. Also gratefully acknowledged are previous publishers, Mosaic Press and Oberon Press, for permission to reprint poems in the selected section.

The publisher gratefully acknowledges the Canada Council for the Arts and the Ontario Arts Council for their generous support.

Wolsak and Wynn Publishers Ltd.
Post Office Box 316
Don Mills, Ontario, Canada M3C 2S7

Canadian Cataloguing in Publication Data

Sherman, Kenneth, 1950
  New and Selected Poems

Poems.
ISBN 0-919897-73-8
I.   Title.

PS8587.H3863W44 2000   C811',54   C00-930599-8
PR9199.3.S53W44 2000

For Marie, Justine, and Adam

Contents

NEW POEMS

A VIEW

I sit on the ancient pier
watching patches of mist
lift from the lake
like ghosts reluctant to go.
Down below – the mysterious stirrings
amidst rocks and old bottles,
abandoned anchors that once held fast,
lost goggles that helped someone see.
In a short while the ghosts will have
disappeared and I'll make out the distant
opalescent island – a place I dreamt of
paddling to when I was a boy
and did once but found nothing
spectacular, except a view
of where I'd come from which was
unexpected and worth the time
it had taken. But the deep –
that's different. I've been there
with my mask, tube, rubber fins –
the ridiculous non-fish –
but no matter how much I've taken in
there's something that I've missed.
It's not only the unpredictable schools
passing through but the landscape itself:
murky, mossy, both growing and decomposing –
a silent richness we're meant to visit,
not inhabit. This pier
juts to where the water
would be over my head,
to where I can see the flags of the distant
marina, clearly. I should be content
with the sun and breeze.
I should wave to those boats
setting off in different directions.

THE DRAWING

She is working in the garden,
her hair held back in a concentrated bun,
face half in shade, half-illumined.
She leans forward to reconsider
a leaf's contour, anther's pollen,
amends with her eraser

then starts again by circling her intent,
ghost movements of a pencil
half inch above paper.
The garden is a season, transient,
and she is rapt, undivided, oblivious
to bird call, rustle, soprano

from the neighbour's radio.
She is working the chiaroscuro
to render this flower, to give us
the resolute grey and white measure.
It will serve as a token
after the obliteration of snow.

LIFTING THE PATIO STONES

Sow bugs and pale worms
no longer than an inch
traversing time's imprint –

those ridges and indentations
formed by the concrete's
crude underside.

Also, you find
a broken barrette,
a small toy mirror

that once fit into the hand of a doll
and a marble the colour
of blue sky –

emblems of someone's childhood,
unclaimed in your open hand,
value undetermined.

Wherever she is,
she won't need these
now,

but close your eyes
and you can hear her,
teasing the others.

BEE BALM

Their petals are a deep red
set off against green leaves
and the white astilbes
planted next to them in your painter's garden.

You said they were curative –
a remedy for heart's disease,
a prescription
to work against dejection.

The ancients would say they grew
from a lover's wound,
or drifted up from the underworld –
spirits vivid but speechless.

Strange to think such colour
rose out of darkness,
nourished by nothing more
than see-through water and light.

Now that their tufts
have shriveled and fallen
all that remains is that alliteration
I first heard on your lips.

RIFT

The silence between the two of them
is not the silence before creation
but what comes after the vessels have been broken.

It is not the speechlessness of animals
nor the muteness of departed souls
but is read in the eyes of the inconsolable.

THE GARDEN

Not one of those casual layouts
that lines a thousand suburban yards
nor one of those professional affairs
too tasteful, manicured, and uninspired,
replicated in a host of homes
that go vacant all summer,
their owners off to Europe
or costly cottages. This garden,
not grandiose or too refined,
was developed slowly by her
and him. It has seen them through
the worst of it, taken them out of themselves
into a space not only fragrant
and colourful, but inspirational
to the ear: Ozark Sundrops,
Russian Sage, Nanking Cherry,
and by the rear French doors,
screens of Boston Ivy. A world
no doubt has been created here,
nothing less, yet one that shows itself
fewer months than it spends
in abeyance: curled brown and crusted,
then anticipatory under snow.
It will not rise without labour.
I have watched its creators
sit on a stone bench and sip water
looking out upon what is good
and noted that as looks left them
and age furrowed their faces,
the garden appeared no less vibrant
though it had no pretence of permanence,
did not resist time
but was a reconciliation with passages,
a forgiveness of flesh. I watched
the two of them admiring it
and the wind brought the fragrance over
as if it knew nothing of fences.

A SUNFLOWER

The ragged sunflower
grown from a seed
that was tossed casually
by the rusted fence
in this chance, unweeded garden
of petals and debris

has made it through chaos
and neglect
to follow the steps of the sun

                in expectation

AT THE BUTTERFLY CONSERVATORY

Their wings are shards of stained glass
or darkness

punctuated by a solitary gem.
Their origin is fire.

Unpredictable, they float
hypnotic as an infant's mobile,

break with eye-blinking flutter
into intricate dart and swerve

then vanish – blend into leaf pattern,
network of stems.

Luminous, other-than-us,
they alight and feed from plants

with bright nomenclature –
Dwarf Flame, Earth Star.

They signal what is near
and far.

TOURING THE BREAD FACTORY

Vats of filtered water. Liquid eggs.
The dough trough, the proof box,
the room of fermentation.

From the sidelines I watched it
mixed and moulded
and placed in pans that were placed

on the belt of creation.
Off to the incessant ovens.
And those shift-workers

in vanilla aprons and caps,
their eyebrows and lashes
dusted by the grace of flour.

The whole humming structure
smelled intimate and sacred.
I felt as if I were an inductee

in the fluorescent temple of Ceres,
and departed, renewed and radiant,
cradling a warm loaf.

STRANGE SEDIMENT

Sunshine refracted through water in the pool
casts a chain-mail pattern of light
on the blue sides and bottom –

a possible net for the swimmer
who tries this depth
discovering a lost hair band,

particles of leaves, strange sediment,
though most entranced
by the shimmering net

that he reaches to grasp,
and finds his hand touching nothing
but illumined.

NIGHT HOCKEY

The rink, freshly flooded
under a single lamplight,
showed our schoolboy shadows.
The boards, weathered and warped,
echoed with the crack of the puck.

That echo carried off
into darkness. In minutes
the ice was scarred, crosshatched:
A strange calligraphy,
the black tape on our sticks –

like perfectly wound phylacteries.
No shin guards, no kneepads,
no helmets (cockiness or
faith?) no referees or ultimate
judgement. Only our squabbling,

jests and minor injuries,
our bonding and levelling.
Games are always more than what
they seem: breakaway, goal,
or chances checked,

winners and losers.
But above us there was the mute
winter sky
and the stars that burned,
regardless.

SANDLOT BALL

I

Fists climb up the shaft of the bat.
Then one of the captains crowns it
with a flattened palm or with fingers
clenched like a crow's talons
while the rest of us look on, expectant,
wanting to be chosen
and please God, not picked last.

II

The auspicious diamond: a sun-drenched stage.
Diving for the ball – the heroic mid-air moment.
The sweetly hit long ball over the fence
or the missed ball, the wide fan and the long walk
back to the bench, past the silent gauntlet
where eyes avoid yours and a friend
gives you a compensating pat.

III

Lessons in life? Are things that white
and black, either failure or eminence?
But keep it all in perspective – after all
it's not the majors, not even the minors,
just sandlot ball, not a lot at stake.
It ought to be pleasurable. Then why
that repeating dream
of the unforgivable error,
or the other where you whack
the bases-loaded homer,
run with an assured, casual gait
and doff your cap to the deafening cheers?

HANDBALL

His deft hand pawed the ball
as it rebounded off walls
streaked with dark tails of comets.

From the upper gallery
I watched him and his partner,
the grace of their unpredictable ballet

and heard the squeal
of sneakers on hardwood, the authoritative
smack of rubber, the blunt calling of the score.

After forty years of competition
two of his fingers were gnarled
from banging and breakage.

Some evenings he'd return,
content that he'd beaten a man much younger.
Other times he'd sulk in the rawness of defeat.

But three times a week he was religiously there,
in the echoing court, testing his reflex and speed
against the immutable law of ageing.

If I were to find his old handball glove,
remnant of what he loved,
I know that its leather

once burnished alive with sweat and wear
would be dried out, curled,
and withered.

Instead, let me be left with the rush
and thud of those soles on hardwood.
And with the calling of the score.

BABEL'S DIARY – 1920

(for Adam Fuerstenberg)

He adopted the name Lyutov – fierce one –
to disguise he was a chosen son
and rode with Cossacks, carbines aslant across their backs.

He, the double-man, both witness and party scribe,
whose secret pages, resurrected,
open to the repeated injunction – *Describe.*

Far from his violin lessons, far from
the genial cadence of Odessa's merchants,
his prose broke staccato like his clattering tachanka

flying over fractured Polish roads:
The dreadful field, sown with mangled men …
Jettisoned notebooks, leaflets, Bibles,

bodies amid the wheat. Standing
before a desecrated ark, he read his fate
on the bullet-pocked synagogue wall

and watched fog rise like ghost-spumes
from the forest of Dubno. There,
momentarily turning from the war,

he set out to find an apiary,
the dark and fragrant honey
concealed somewhere in that shaded depth,

then wrote,
Remember the dead of Dubno.
Describe the forest.

NOTES

I like to travel backward from the blast
of Wynton Marsalis

into the studio on February 16, 1934
and hear Pops play "The Peanut Vendor,"

that detestable Cuban rumba:
"Forget the song," he'd say "but listen to my notes."

Luxurious weeds of New Orleans,
sun's reflection off blown brass,

and the notes, compressed, climbing
out of a delinquent school, a ragman's soprano,

reverberation of a wash basin –
first heard on my father's scarred 78s,

carried all the way from Storyville
to a bungalow in mid-town Toronto –

not far given the speed of his riffs, his gliss,
his scat: the conviction

of his gravel intonation.
Who is this man? I asked,

seen on Sullivan when I was six,
so unglamorous with disfigured lip

eyes bulging comedic ("You dawg!")
ubiquitous white handkerchief mopping sweat

("Chocolate drop, that's me …")
the heaviness of his hue.

O quarters, quadrilles, quadroons.
Dance of the Bamboula

and voodoo: Satchelmouth, Dippermouth,
Rivermouth, Gate.

The blue notes gelling
in the fatherless emptiness,

in the knowledge of his mother's
necessary hustle,

then swung into joyousness
on the floor of Lulu White's palatial brothel.

At Black Benny's funeral.
In Funky Butt Hall.

THE DRIVER

(for Seymour Mayne)

Early morning, I'd hear him
drive up the gravel path
to the cottages, his rusted van
with the simple block lettering –
COHEN'S BAKERY.
Once we'd appeared
he'd open the back doors slowly
as if a ceremony was about to begin.

Before the sun burnt off the morning mist
or soaked up the wetness
from the untamed blades
of country grass, I was
taking in the heady waft of chocolate
Danishes, apricot squares.

And then he was packaging them,
arranging each order with care,
taking our money with a nod
of appreciation,
placing it diffidently
in the pockets of his apron.

Late at night I'd find myself
thinking of him, knowing
he'd soon be leaving the city,
setting out through summer darkness,
barrelling north along the hushed highway
carrying the loaded silver trays,
the stacks of unconstructed boxes
each white as the unwritten page.

27

FISHING WITH RED

Early morning.
you tap gently on my bedroom window
and in a minute I'm dressed, a boy of twelve
helping you pack the trunk of your Buick
with stringer, net, Shakespeare rods, and tackle box.
At Bonnie Boats we untie the utility
and cut a small wake across clear water.
No one else out there. When we come to your special spot
I let out the anchor and the water we passed through
settles like a mirror. Re-silvers. Then, as day warms,
I warm to your familiar jokes,
your advice on what size hook to use, which lure,
how far to play bait from the bottom.
In the cool plastic container the leeches
expand and contract like rubber bands
while your radio plays "old man's" music –
Vic Damone, Tony Bennett. If I suggest Chuck Berry,
you declare he would only scare the fish.
That was thirty-five years ago, Red,
when you were my cottage neighbour
in floppy blue hat, flies on the band,
a man without pretence or affectation,
whose sons disliked fishing as much as my father did
and so we found ourselves as stand-ins.
I want you to know I still send out lines,
though what I come up with is harder to weigh
than those grey bass gaping incredulous
on the stringer you'd hold arm high.
Little did we know that what I was taking in
those mornings would serve as preparation:
your abrupt silence when you felt a quivering, then a tug,
and focussed wholly on the line's tension
or your calm, soft-spoken patience when nothing happened
and it seemed that an absence had swallowed everything
in the cold, verdant depths.

THE WELL

One summer at the cottage when I was seven or eight
we listened to our radio as they broadcast live
the rescue attempt of a boy who'd fallen
down a dried-out well. I went to bed
but found it hard to fall asleep
hearing the muted voice of the newscaster
coming from our living room
and thinking of that boy, my age,
trapped in a darkness more terrifying
than the darkness that surrounded my bed.
I realized then that you could be with someone
and imagine his fear without having to endure it
to the end. It went on for two or three days.
When news came that they'd got him out
but that it had been too late, I noted how we all
spoke quietly over breakfast,
as if there had been a death in our family.
By afternoon our voices were normal again.
Then the newspapers appeared with a photo
of the stretcher, the rescue workers, the bowed heads.
There was an insert photo of the parents:
they looked like dirt farmers, poor locals.
Why hadn't they covered that unused well?
Were they unable to envision catastrophe?
Were they fatalists? Is that what I read
in their gaunt faces: in his frayed overalls,
in her cheap cotton dress? The well was there
waiting to happen: If it was to happen to them and theirs
so be it. Or maybe the boy had not stumbled in.
Maybe he was overly inquisitive, or even leapt
with that dark urge that grows in each one of us.
How many times had he and his siblings
run laughing by that well? I walked behind our cottage.
We too had a well no longer in use.
It was covered with a circular slab of concrete.

It would take a machine to raise it. Or a powerful giant.
I imagined him bearded and solemn,
rolling the circular slab like a crude wheel
along dirt roads and over voiceless farm fields
leaving behind the inexplicable well.

DISCOVERY

You wanted a private death, far from the curious,
where your body, turned to bone,
would be a whiteness that atoned for whatever
darkness led you there. The police could not determine
where you'd gone and safely pushed your case aside,
but we could not accept your disappearance
since it questioned our very lives. A private eye
was sent to find you out. He discovered you
cleansed within the shadow of a hard maple,
protected from the searching sun.
The space inside your skull was buzzing
with a myriad of winged brilliant things
where previously there had been only their phantoms.

THE MORE THINGS CHANGE

Some things never change.
They're deep inside. As for the rest –
nothing in this city has stayed the same.
And your childhood town by the lake –
unrecognizable. The wharf and the boat
named "Lucky Draw" – gone.

Memory has them.
But don't walk down that street
where your house used to be
or pass the vacant lot
where the two of you first kissed.
Whatever buildings are there, they're spaces.

A CANADIAN ON SANIBEL ISLAND

(for Eric Ormsby)

There were thousands of tiny seashells
in the sand that glistened
like chips of porcelain. That was the home
of the brown pelican, of the egret
who takes minutes to decide a single step,
and of the grinning alligator, submerged,
mistaken for a log.

The sun there thickened my blood,
made me motionless.
Its light was diffuse, generous,
not the hard, focussed
glare of our northern sky. And I thought
of my countrymen
two thousand kilometres north,

testing the icy pavements,
dreading the vast distances,
gathering nerve to counter the cutting winds.
To feel at home I had to imagine a point
beyond the parasols and beach chairs
where there'd be no sound but the droning waves
and no one to read my footprints.

ON A TOURIST BEACH NEAR BOMBAY

The tanned and topless
from the West
with their parasols, their novels,
their spiritual eclipse.
Now and then they peer
above their sunglasses
to see a sky that for them
is blue, banal, and limitless.
Along the beach a stick-man
dressed in white sarong
is walking, cradling
his case of metal instruments.
He is an ear-cleaner.
(This is a profession in the East.)
He speaks a different tongue,
stands silently
offering creased letters
of recommendation,
his eyes patient as sand.
He moves gently
like a mid-day shadow
collecting a curt or silent refusal
from each sullen, broiling body.
He has come to clean out ears
expecting there to be someone
who wants to hear
the urgent waves,
the insistent wind.

UP THERE

You're up there
in what you'd call
the middle of nowhere, midst
spruce, cedars, ferns, and firs –
all those green words,
and only a hint of the human
with that weathered deck
leading out into the lake,
the reflective surface at sunset
returning the self
you thought you'd lost.
When you're back on the highway,
numb from the hyphenated distance,
or down here finally, on the thick
and charmless pavement,
your identity dissipating amongst
traffic, gossip, the tedious and the needless –
recall the solidness of the rock
on which you sat, its rough certitude,
the trenchant silence that opened you
and the heron that flew through,
unhurried and solemn,
confirming your direction.

35

BUYING AN EXCELLENT BOOK FOR $1.99

It seems no one wanted to read this.
A black marker
was run across the bottom
to say what's inside
is almost worthless.

A fringe of sullen beige
at the edge of the paper
is creeping in
threatening to mar the clarity
of the vision.

The binding has hardened
from lack of human touch.
Still it seems committed
to hold together
the elements.

Time has sat like salt on the words.
Some have been preserved
while others were eaten away

to where a light shines
through the page.

SELECTED POEMS

37

BEE-KEEPING

(for Lyle)

The bees are at peace
with their maze of wax and brood,
their crazy labour and sweetening swarm.

Chairman of the board
I inspect their habitual industry.
Safe in my astronaut's get-up
I gloat at the sealed sunny cells,
the overtime muttering.

Then like the cartoon bear
pursued by the furious squadron
I lumber away one guilty frame.

Their heated buzzing saws the brain.
Kamikaze, some leave
their pulsing barbs behind
as I kneel to razor the wax caps,
induce the flow.

I am licking the sweetness
from my hands, bare now.
The remaining few
like a baby's mobile
circle my head lazily.
Their plaintive drone fades.
They will return
to work for me.

JERUSALEM MARKET

Near some station of the cross
a shop offers animal heads
piled in pyramids.

Infant pink and white
they illuminate
the violet dusk.

Their wide grins
bring to mind the manger beasts
whose supplicating flesh

now marketable, skinned,
hangs from hooks or
revolves on roasting sticks.

"Hot *shwarma*," cries the butcher's son.
A pilgrim herd halts
to feed and to forgive.

MY FATHER KEPT HIS CATS WELL FED

In back of the tailor shop
far from consumer eye
they'd stretch
on thick rolls of mohair,
on new blue synthetics from Japan.

And somehow he bought time
to keep fresh milk in the saucepan,
providing leftovers
from a hurried lunch.

Between the measurements and complaints,
between the clean sound of closing shears
they were his own animal symphony
purring at a conducted stroke
under the chin,
behind the ear.

The cats,
they sang my father's praise
in the fishbone throat of the coldest nights
where their lives, once lean,
curled fat and secure

and dreamt their gifted names:
No-Neck, Schvartz Katz, Rabinovitz ...
a regular *minyan*
to greet his early mornings
when snow outside
dropped soft as padded paws
and the shop was a museum hush.

There they reclined,
impenetrable as the sphinx,
the curious engines of their soft throats
running, their great eyes smouldering
in the precious twilight of my father's day

before the startling ring
and the long unwinding of curses
and cloth.

SUMMER IN OLD FOREST HILL

These are the homes where pets die better
than men in lesser districts,
where a new recipe for ratatouille
is the day's hot news.

Wiry Mediterraneans come to cut the lawn:
uncultivated Chatterly lovers, under the lunch-time
foreign maple tree they sit bewildered,
imagining what power hums behind chipped stone and mortar.

From the pool's pump such sweetness flows:
the children's privileged glee
as their rich-brown bodies
cannonball the turquoise deep:

iced tea for auntie and the live-in's rural smile.
A young wife sips her green aperitif,
the half-read *Feminine Mystique*
straddling her naked thigh.

The flutter of affairs is what
dispels her boredom; that
and the troubles with charwomen
murmured into phones antique.

RIMBAUD'S WATERWHEEL

On his mother's farm in Roche
they sigh relief at his departure,
resume their sunny pious toil
as in a canvas by Millet:
the kerchiefs and bulging calves
of women gleaning,
brawny men scattering seed –
an idyll soon to be mocked.

In his hometown of Charleville
the square still swells with regiments:
handlebar mustachios
grind out marching sermons
to which pretty parasols
and stiff miniature flags
pop up
            and down.

Beyond them now
he reclines on the deck of a steamer.
Flies quiver in a halo
about his totem of festering leg.
He burns fever,
focuses on the diamond sweat
glistening on the upper lip
of the young boy he will sell.

Behind the waterwheel
pale reeds glitter like knives
while the river breaks with
what always lurked below:
gnarled head of hippo
unhinging his fatal yawn,
the croc's saw jaw
feeding a cynical grin,
while on the bank, blacks,

their ghostly robes billowing,
haul crates of carbines
into the indignant bush.

It is a new order
that churns in the waterwheel.
The railing's paint gives way
like crusted blood as the trader
leans to watch his face
fold in the gelatinous green,

the sun ball above his head

      another head

O from a forgotten poem.

45

FAIRY TALES

The fairy tales have no easy endings.
Hansel and Gretel do not go home.
And that spidery wart of a witch,
that black-laced bitch who waits
in the woods of sly-eyed rodents
and owls who rotate their conspiring heads
has a thousand and one sugared plans
to keep you here and in pain.

In the stinking saw-tooth dungeon
of her face your gingerbread dreams
dissolve. The family members will cook
one another alive (for love,
they say, for love). And the dove
who once returned you safe and sound
is now a crow, sniggering
on the home's thatched eaves.

There is no reconciliation. The longer
you stay the more sluggish your feet
the heavier your lids while your brain
begins defending those rusted chains
of fear. Nor is there a hunter near
with glimmering axe, waiting for
your sobs, waiting to rush in and
split the hag's dry pod of a head.

Stealth, my dearest: childhood is over.
Put away your green balloon and slam
the oven door. The smell of her sizzling
flesh is not so bad as you imagined.
Later, in the blue bruise of forest
you will leave your sister,
whisper your own name over and over.
You will lie down and sleep
beneath the clear and separate stars.

A PSALM OF THE ELEPHANT MAN

What protrudes from my upper jaw
what makes of my mouth a shattered clam
a tortured vent.

My speech is indistinct,
                              my vowels rise

like wild birds,
                    my consonants grind

and splutter
                    like an engine's damaged

gears,
          my peculiar limp
                              beats time.

This is the song of thy suffering servant.
This is the articulation of the New Age.
This is God's hobbling little poem.

I drone on in His image.

INTO THE WORKHOUSE

The drunk, the old,
those poor through injury
            through lunacy

the young unwed women
who are pregnant –

runs in the new social fabric
the tireless shining engines weave.

Then there is me.
                A doctor once remarked
had I not had this affliction
I would have been good looking.

Behind the bulging bone, the bales
of skin,
            can you see
me?

My left arm has gone untouched.
It is the one visible part of which I am proud.
As the rest grows thicker and thicker,
                                    it seems
thinner, a child's limb,
                a branch
off the tree in Eden.

                When the bell rings
I put down my mallet
                and limp
into the dining hall where even the most
ravenous put down their spoons

            raise disbelieving eyes.

DECEMBER 25, 1880

It is Christmas in the workhouse.
All of London is still.
A fine drizzle falls.

You can smell the dinner
they are preparing for us:
pork, plum pudding – a heavenly
break from our daily bowl of "hell-broth."

Even the more manic lie in their beds
silent, contemplating the grey light
that sifts down from high, murky windows.

I have kept count:
over the past six months I have unravelled
hemp amounting to 1500 pounds, tearing
strands thin as hair from old ropes,
my hands blistering maggot white.

Would that make enough for a new rope
I could wrap about the equator,
I wonder what they'll do if my hand
gets much thicker,
                    my body
a breathing tuber
only to be watered?

In the cobblestone courtyard
men in navy blue uniforms,
eye-stained, reeking of gin,
stand guard over our tree

silvered and glittering.

A PRETTY LADY

It became a cult among the personal friends
of the Princess to visit the Elephant Man.

Treves brought her in, it was a coolish spring day.
She smiled, she wore a mauve dress, I could
hear the hem of it as she crossed the room,
it was the sound of water.

I was wood, I was part of my chair. When she
took my hand and said, "So happy to make
your acquaintance"
                    I cried.

Some men want the world. I only want to be
lovable.
            Am I lovable? Is there a shudder
of eros
            in all this wattled ugliness?

The countesses, the actresses, the Princess Alexandra –

I have all their photographs,
                            signed,
                                    smiling at me
from atop my dark commode.

                            After we have chatted,
exchanged pleasantries, views on literature,

                            they leave
                            (they always leave).

I claw the air
            where their perfume
                        lingers.

THE WORD

One day you will know
it was not neuro-fibro-
matosis,
        nor any of your other
damned specimens of language.

Rather, it was the word
I could not sing.

        Once I tried
and someone taped a pound note to my lips.
I tore it off and the monstrous hiss of
the engines drowned me out.

What's the use, I thought, watching
men leave whole each morning,
return in the dark like small change.

So I held in the word
but the consonants
        battered against my palate,
fell back flattened and dull as worked metal.

Those few words that escaped
were thin wind
        down a stinking mineshaft.

The word tried new exits,
        blasting bone,
pushing out these pendulous folds

till I became the abc of pain
till I became the sound
        skewered through flesh

straining
        with the terror of an epic.

TAKING THE TOUR AT AUSCHWITZ

The tour guide was old, bent,
very thin with long grey hair.

He led us into the basement
of one of the administrative offices.
There, in the dim light, two skulls
the Nazis had placed side by side:
one of a rabbi, one of a priest.

"Martyrs," the tour guide said.
"They were hanged with piano wire
till it cut through their necks.
Their bodies were fed to the dogs."

After he had finished,
the two skulls began to groan:
"*Oy*" cried one.
"My Lord in Heaven," cried the other.

"What in the world could make them
cry out still?" asked a member
of our tour.
                    Just then the shelf
on which the skulls were placed split.
The two skulls fell to the ground
and shattered with a loud crack.

"You see," said the tour guide
nodding his old grey head.
"Nothing, nothing is definitive:
and to suffering and evil
there is no end."

BEFORE MY WEDDING

I am in the kitchen
talking softly
with Louis and John.

Dark suits, pale
carnations.

This morning
we permit ourselves
to touch
like women

we straighten
one another's silk
bow-tie.

DECEMBER 24

Silent night, our furnace whirrs.
On my way to bed I stop
outside my daughter's door,
her breath
the rhythm of a small sea.

Outside, stars
burn like splinters of ice,
smoke out of chimneys
coils through the mute
and endless dark.

I will wait another moment
listening
for my daughter's breath
before I turn out the light.

YOU CAN DO SOMETHING ABOUT THE WAY YOU LOOK
(lifted from the New York Times Magazine, October 26, 1980)

Are your eyes saggy,
puffy?
They needn't be.

How is your chin?
Slimming down
or reconstructing it
is very do-able.

Noses are also changeable.
You don't have to live with yours
if you don't think it's terrific.

Remember,
ears shouldn't be
too noticeable.
Are yours?

How is your face in general?
Wrinkled?
Put your hands at your temples
and push up
and back.
Now,
don't you look better?

Dear Creative Surgery Centre:
I want to look as young as I feel.
Please send me more information

Or call 832-3028
now
for consultation.

FOUR FIGURES FROM THE FALL

The serpent is curled tightly
about the branch of a tree, an oily
blackish green,
waiting;
his face is expressionless, his lidless eyes
are glass.

Eve stares out of the canvas
in innocence, as if unaware of her body
below the neck. Her breasts,
a mottled yellow tempera,
are small, hard, and flat
but her hips are extremely large
as if she is already pregnant.

Adam is muscular, compact,
yet hunched as if shrinking
from his possible cosmic proportions.
He is reaching toward Eve
as she extends one hand
toward the tree
and its serpent.

To the left an angel or demiurge
with a cleft sword and childlike eyes
looks on with apprehension.

Everything is in a state
of suspension, as if the painter
had wished to hold time,
had convinced himself of a power
over death,
as if he were unaware
that everything in his painting
had already happened.

ADAM NAMES THE BEAST

He is making the animals,
scoops mud, blows into it:
what comes is fur,
udder, talon, paw

faster than balloons
blown at a carnival

then He passes them on
to me
for naming:

I call you giraffe
I call you hippopotamus

After a time, I suggest
another process:

I'll provide the names
and see what shapes
You come up with.

But He refuses.
First the flesh, He says,
then the language.

I envy His hands of mud
and blood. He is a doer. I
come after.
                  You can't change the order,
He says, but you'll try
with your syntax, your syllables,
your truncated vocables –
face it, you are disparate
and complex.

He retreats and night comes
and in the darkness I see
that I was made in such a way
as to question
reality.
      I dream
and therefore I can be
deceived.
         I love
         I love

I disappear
back
into the earth

but my naming is endless.

FLIP SIDE

In that world Adam is saved from himself,
Eve kneels below the bower and sings each evening
to the expressionless head of a serpent
who laps from a pool of milk
which is really moon's reflection –
everyone laughs at such illusions

in that world the masses read poetry
that is about red grapes, the fragrance of flesh,
you and I appear as quickly as imagined characters
and take our place between the lion and the lamb –
when I brush my hand over your breast
your nipple rises and caresses the soft centre
of my palm, not like a nail but like the snail
which is known for its slowness

there is enough time here for everyone, no-one
has seen his own death, no-one feels diminished,
the boy thinks of his sex not as a blade
but as a flower rising red between the legs
the girl releases all the stars
from her darkness, she has no fear,
no-one lurks in corners, no-one is captive
in cellars

the angels and the devils dance, knowing
they're in costume, exchanging masks

water at times turns to ice and does not mind

wine becomes urine and flows back
into the clots of humus and new shoots
grow

everything is flexible, all the wonders
have been seen before but nothing is a bore,
nothing seems used or old, everything flows
as in a stream, as in a dream

59

OVER

I flew above the smog and dust.
I had a bird's view
of the planet, its history, heartbreaking,
reduced to a pinpoint, a small
present:
        Egypt dead, Rome dying,
Athens broken, Soviet satellites, America
its colonies.

The globe, so tired of spinning
with its monuments
that all squat now, meaningless,
kitsch,
        so dizzy
from its shifting languages, its horns,
its static, its network of Muzak,
its winnowing jets.

The sunset was smearing
over large-scale death, black
branches, no regeneration
to speak of.
            If only we could stop
and put everything back again.

The world is not a poem, I reminded
myself, it is not an exercise
in perfection.
            Create, I said, be
joyous against the blare, the wholesale
flux
        make what light you can
        from the chaos.

MESSIAH

He is a function
of our highest imagination
but believe me,
he was never
wholly present.

In each of us
a small part of him
and a large portion
of the opponent.

Not one man, not one
reaching, but a striving
to turn the blight
into mercy, to turn the bloodied hands
to blessing.

As for the great father:
he has imploded
and his absence beckons,
it draws us in.

Despite the heaps of bodies
that we photograph daily
and under whose weight we feel powerless
it is not too late to love, to practise
gentleness,
to speak beyond the darkness,
to fill the void
with our voice.

If and when he comes
it will only be
to sign the one poem
all of us have written.

JACKSON'S POINT

The town's promontory tongue,
it juts into Lake Simcoe
making a division:

to the west there is the protected bay
where a benevolent wind
skims taut sails

and where swimmers breaking surface
laugh, conjuring my own
childhood splashers.

The other side is whitecapped,
a vociferous blue-black,
a snarl of weather.

Today I sit on the weather side
in a cottage that is deserted,
watching through the window

as a ritual circle of boys
on the other
on the bayside pier

swing a girl
in choral countdown
and heave her into deep water.

I put my pen to white paper.

Carry me, tenuous sail,
to that community
of splashers

and to the voice
of a girl
caught in mid-air.

GOLDMAN

Gruff, bearded,
before beards were fashionable, he sat,
Jack's giant on a doll's stool,
his belly buddhistic,
before the pyramids of thick-skinned oranges,
plums a fathomless indigo blue.

An anxiety of fruit flies haloed his head
as he pulled from his pocket
a soiled white remnant
to swab his creased and shimmering neck.
By his feet, scattered peach pits,
each deep and furrowed –
a brain's integral convolutions.

And what was time then to this Goldman
who sat in the sun watching summers
exchange the horse-drawn wagon
for a Chevy van,
the privy at his cottage
give way to plumbing,
mirroring faucets:

his sweet spoiling pyramids,
his outdoor personality
and complex Yiddishisms
given over to storefront minimal sign, glass,
refrigeration's monotone hum.

DIVINER

(For Dennis Hayes)

He'd come to find our well.
I recall his floppy fisherman's hat,
hooks and feathered flies
strung along the band,
his gauntness, his silence,
as if words would mar his focus
on the sweet, magnetic
undercurrent.

And his forked, unassuming branch,
his stuttering steps
over the sea-green grass

almost clownish.

                  I watched, hesitant
about believing
in his life of finding,
his innuendoes

of other worlds.
His clenched hands, tanned, bronzed,
seemed permanent
but the veins bulged thick
as bloated worms.

Drama of the downpull:
for a moment the look upon his face
sent shivers.
               Then it was over.

We paid him.

He drank half a glass of water
and was gone.

A CIRCLE SONG FOR THOMSON

Each summer Thomson came
to jack up the back of our cottage.
Each summer he'd stand with my father,

take off his hat, scratch his head,
stare at the columns of concrete blocks
sunk deeper into the ground.

"Yup," he'd finally say (he'd
say it every summer). "Gotta
jack 'er up, add more blocks."

Each summer Thomson grew older.
Each summer our cottage sank further.

The cottage still stands.
Thomson lies deeper.

CLEANING FISH

Mrs. Ellis, survivor, the blue numerals
stitched on your forearm,
drawing my eyes
to where they shouldn't stare.

Noon, you'd sit at the cedar picnic-table
with your nephew's morning catch;
the corrugated shears to clip fins,
the thin blade

you ran along white bellies;
the gentle lessons
you provided
on anatomy:

"This, the liver. This,
the heart." Green and red
they tumbled out
like gleaming jewels.

I recall your hand
cradling a diaphanous
sack
of pinkish pearls.

"The mamma's eggs," you said,
holding them to the raw August light.
Squinting,
you let out a shrill laugh.

Were you mad,
I sometimes wondered,
thinking of where
you had been.

In the grey galvanized
pail
the floating scales
and fillets

the astonished bass heads
gaping
on newspaper
that had yellowed.

BURROUGH'S HARDWARE, 6 AM

The aroma of cedar and polish.
The canvas knapsacks.
The oiled rifles,
their shining walnut stocks.

Mounted on a wall,
its chestnut eyes gazing, feminine,
the solitary deer's head.
Tackle-boxes. Sinkers. Lures.

And the communion of men
in red flannel jackets,
their gruff
morning voices

their wrists
testing the reflex of casters,
wisps
of white line.

When the sun broke through the storefront's
green translucent blind
it was as if those figures
plunged underwater

where they cast now in my memory
amongst proliferating weeds,
the startled jettisons of crayfish,
blue boulders,

safe from their famished clichés –
the pickerel lost in the attic,
shellacked, mounted
on mahogany veneer.

FRIDAY-NIGHT SERVICES

Walking home down main street,
I catch my reflection
in the window of the hall
where the local toughs

drink and dance.
I am startled to see
that I have forgotten
to remove my skullcap.

PINBALL

Dogs and cherry sodas.
From the speakers of the Wurlitzer in bass-driven mono
came Elvis's quivering "Heartbreak Hotel."

I dropped a thin but potent dime into the slot
and watched *Moon Man* light up. Pulsing stars,
milky astronauts,
the whoosh of meteors and ships.

I loved those rolling, mercurial spheres,
unpredictable off bumpers –
they'd knock the creature-pictured squares
that dropped like tiny tombstones,
zoom from Venus to Pluto
till lost down final corridors
or through the galaxy's black holes.

A voice urged, "Use your flippers, kid, your flippers,"
as the bell-stung numbers rolled and rolled
into the astronomical zeros.

A boy stood watching,
pale, impoverished –
no coins ever rattled in his pockets.
He leaned hard on the machine.

The joyous cacophony droned to a halt
as if swallowed down a tube.

The stars went out on that darkened board
as the red-lettered TILT lit up like an accusation
and the glass gave us back our lonely reflections.

A BARN OF ICE

We brought our lawnmower
needing it fixed,
to the family I'd heard referred to
as bumpkins, country hicks.

We crossed a squall of chickens
in their dry and wasted yard;
amongst the scattered weeds
a heap of rusted auto parts.

A boy was playing jacks
on the peeling, fractured porch;
the obscure figure of his mother
hovered behind the dim screen door.

The boy's face was ingenuous,
a converging mass of freckles
as if someone had splattered him
with melted caramel.

"Wanna see somethin' unusual?" he asked,
walking down to greet me.
By the broken lawnmower
our fathers stood talking.

He led me through the bleaching
heat of that summer's day
to the sagging, splintered barn,
a dead archaic grey.

Yet the hinges squealed loudly
as if the barn door truly lived;
the frigid air that hit us
took away my breath.

It was like plunging under water
and for a time I lost my sight.
Then gradually I discerned
the towering blocks of ice

piled massive, miraculous
like an awesome wedding cake;
the sawdust that preserved it
shimmered like golden flakes.

We stood there in the darkness.
Neither spoke a word.
Then a voice from outside hollered
"Shut the goddamn door!"

I left him there abruptly
and crossed the wasted yard
to where my father in dark glasses
sat waiting in the car.

And passed the strutting rooster's
voracious, scanning eye;
he cocked his head and blinked,
blinked away the light.

BOB ULMER'S HOUSEHOLD

Only three blocks away
my old-world refuge
where language shifted tempo:
Hungarian, to English, to French.

Out of nowhere they'd appear,
those prose-perfect cats – Hemingway,
Fitzgerald – and old Samson
with his gouged owl's neck and badger's body,

his biblical scowl.
One day he left;
six months later you found him
scratching at the milk-box door.

Your younger brother's paint-by-number
Blue Boy, flat and inexact,
hung on the living-room wall.
No plastic-covered sofa there,

no nervousness
about beige carpet,
no breakables
except the human heart.

And I recall your mother's Danube smile,
her necessary Flaubert
on the night-table,
her ex-operatic soprano

displayed between tales of Budapest,
Paris, Tunis:
the flight and persistence
of mid-century Jews.

At the cluttered dining-room table
your grandfather, frail, exotic,
with velvet skullcap, scarlet satin robe,
mused over the world news.

I marveled at his oriental shuffle
when he rose to meet the girls you brought home.
His eyes
would spring alive.

Dear friend, I lounged there
in the decent luxury of domestic chaos,
the wafting scent
of cat-food,

Brahms on the stereo,
comics and books of high calibre
scattered everywhere,
more home to me than home.

COMMUNICADO

This is the simple story of the writer:
there was no one to talk to
at home so he began
to talk to paper.

PEANUT PUPPETS

(for Marie)

Tiny halves of peanut shells – corrugated, wrinkled.
With red and black markers
you sketched on one a dog's face, on the rest
the likenesses of our family members,
your quick strokes cartooning the pocked surface
into a surprised line of vaudeville expressions.
Shreds of felt for dangling basset ears and human hair.
They wagged from the fleshy tips of your fingers
their dumb show of affection.
And who could explain the length to which I loved them,
their sweet meat long gone,
marveling at what is made out of dried husk and pen.

BATHING BEAUTIES, SUNNYSIDE, 1931

Dear Shades, I love the long grainy line of you
with names I imagine like Mabel, June, Dolores.
A few of you, I suspect, are still alive,
but as for your beauty
that overdressed news photographer caught
one August afternoon in his wide, generous lens
(a break from the Great Depression)
it has been given over to others: new lines, new figures.
But how astonishing to be joined to one glorious moment.
And how dreadful: for all portraiture is an entrapment,
and for survivors who totter in the grotesqueries of age,
a hurtful looking-back.
Each and every one of your faces is contemporary:
I've seen you on the streets
if one foregoes the bobbed hair and modest suits
that look like oddly cut long underwear.
Arm-in-arm you pose, classical chorus line,
tender legion of the human, frozen in summer light.
You smile into the moment which,
given knowledge of what comes next,
is perhaps a definition of courage.

WATCHING LAMAS PRAY

Twelve years ago
Red Guards lynched five priests
from this –
The Temple of Universal Tranquility.

These that I see today, barefoot, heads shaven
to skin, are the last of China's lamas.
The others fled, or were slaughtered
in the vast provinces.

I close my eyes and see one on a bicycle
speeding down a country road.
I see the sharpened hoe
and sickle.

I hear the thud,
the desperate wing-like fluttering
of his robe;
the pathetic gurgle of the paddy

as his body
starts its slow descent
through the fathom
of sodden soil.

And these before me now
with their incense, their dissonance
of horns and bells –
are they noble or pitiful

as they lean to their text,
determined to pose again
the dreadful,
ancient questions?

My guide, a ranking cadre,
officious, perplexed, wonders aloud
why I wish to linger here
with what he calls "relics."

Gautama, what name shall I give
that within me
that wishes to enter that faded fresco
on the wall

and stand
eyes closed,
with you
and your huddled disciples?

Not far from here there is a Great Wall
and beyond that a world of transistors and mirrors
where men figure the meaning
of meaning.

It is late in the day. My camera
seems to weigh as much as granite.
When I step outside my shadow is horribly elongated
as if a man had been stretched.

Cheng-de, June 1986

79

SEMINAL CLOTH

In my father's tailor shop
men sewed arms to shoulders,
measured legs as the day drained
to where razors and pins shone in the dimness.
I could hear the flesh-like tearing of thread.

In the box beneath the cutting-table
the material scraps gathered:
sharkskin, hounds-tooth,
herringbone tweed.

As a child, I buried myself in that darkness
beneath the marvelous patterns
and practiced the animal names
until the box became a boat,
the darkness, a sea.

Far off, I could hear
the muffled voice of my father, calling.

FEDORA

On a downtown street corner
near Tip Top Tailors
I find myself
looking for my father.

I pass a darkened hat shop
south on Spadina
that displays a fedora –
the sort he used to wear

in the dead heart of winter
when he'd come home from work
drained, without words.
In the sudden warmth of the house

his glasses fog.
He takes off his coat and his hat
then pours himself
a thimble of Scotch.

Under the bald glare
of a suburban streetlight
our driveway is filling
with snow.

My father eats his late supper
then again puts on
his hat and his coat.
My pillow is next

to my bedroom window
so I can hear
the clear and solitary
scrape of his shovel.

81

The sound slices through me.
What is he shoveling
if not the days
that lie buried

in the banks of whiteness
that will melt
and be carried by wind?
On a closet shelf,

years later, I find
my father's fedora
with its stained sweatband,
the possibility of its soft folds,

its rigid brim.
When I run my hand inside
along the cool satin lining
I can feel the absence.

Somewhere, my father is traveling
with what he could not give.
What he gave
I hold now in my hand.

EARTH-MOVERS

One summer I worked at my uncle's tire factory
watching an endless stream of shiny black tires
roll onto transport trucks. To my uncle,
they appeared as impressive zeros
strung out after a dollar sign and digit.
Some were the height of an African elephant
and were used on mining machines
called earth-movers. My uncle's salesman,
John Hoffmayer, drove a black Toronado
into northern Quebec to sell them to mining executives
who sat in prefab heated cabins,
dressed in warm cardigans, sipped warm rum
and told jokes about women.

I myself learned to load the monster tires.
As long as you kept them moving
you were okay. In motion they could be balanced
which to me seemed indicative of the system.
If you stopped to consider them
they would topple over, threatening
to crush you to death.

All that summer, the sky
looked grey through the dusty skylight
of my uncle's factory, the men's flesh
pale and drained
against the sombre blue overalls.
We were making tires
for machines that would snort, whine,
and claw deep into the earth's belly
while our days were rolling:
my summer days
passing one after the other
out of the great circular moulds
with the monotony of black, shiny zeros.

A BLACK BOOK

Burnt heart, seared letters whose serifs
almost touch

against a whiteness, a void expanse,
polar terror of the limitless.

Its creator departed, not missed,
an instrument whose gut once resounded

with the flux of his time, whose larynx flexed
against time – this, its deposit.

Once it threatened to swallow
the world it invented

but brought it back out of wreckage,
scarred, intact.

Between stiff covers, it scowls
with the scorn of the neglected

chords its empathy for the torn,
feeds off its dreams,

nurtures its rock, its frayed leaves
go on growing.

Postulates wholeness,
beginning and end,

but is strong in its knowledge
that this is illusion.

For some, a comfort
though not its intent

what it wishes now
more than to be read

is to wrestle each comer
down into its depths

into the blinding belly of its lastness.
Those who surface

are ash-eyed, born
from their breakage

whole image out of negative

dark fruition of the press.

SIEVE

What passes through it
is always more than air.
Fluid of our lives, a moment's density
that weighs upon the handle
then pours down the sink like a prayer –

panic in the pipes,
a running anxiety
under the pitch
of the metropolis.

Once the earth was a sieve –
what passed through it
nourished.

In the night sky, that colander
of stars, those punctures of darkness,
implosion of black gas,
what the texts term "dark matter"

drawing you into curved air,
an endless returning
where your hands are shining, fluorescent
like the pale limbs of amphibians
or fetal creatures, potential,
there.

THE ESCHATOLOGY OF BEES

The striped prisoner's uniform
of bees,
          their monotony, their industry,
the terror of their hives.

Whose life do they live there,
with the others?
Their frenetic sound, electrical,
like some transformer
taken to its limit

though too profound for that.

They swarm in clouds,
jittery, atomic
about the brooding branches
of the tree.
Their layered homes
look shaggy, woven,
almost biblical.

Is it their hum
their drone of lamentation
that has me focus on my shadow
frozen
on the gravel road?

I razor the combs
and raise the structured cells
to my lips

knowing what they make is sweet
though they speak
of final things.

HALLOWE'EN PUMPKIN

I brought it to decompose
by the fence in our backyard garden
and watched it rot through foul November,
its deepening orange, a molten, setting sun.

For weeks it held the shock of human expression
amongst the ordinary sparrows and squirrels
with its mouth's round note of astonishment
and its star-shaped eyes, charred and mournful.

The stem from its head
which had served as a handle to open
that night of candles and masks
had withered into the dry worm of a question.

Its dark absence of ears
now led to a riddling where.
And I could see into its future
all blanketed by white powder

gradually greeting the compost of April,
ready for our birth garden
though what it would bring forth
would be beauty, not invention.

And peering into its hollow spaces
I recalled the quick eyes of the children
that night by the harvest table,
the determined lines they sketched on flesh.

TREASURE OF THE SIERRA MADRE

An unshaven foreigner
begs for quarters
in a small town
which is always on the border.

Hatch a scheme
or invent a plot:
three men, their pickaxes, canteens, canvas,
tin pans, suspicions, lust.

"No one gets the best of Fred C. Dobbs."
The paranoiac eyes of Bogart flare
in this desert fable
unfolding in film noir's stark chiaroscuro.

Machetes, sombreros.
The maniacal bray of a burro.
The gold-capped laugh of a bandito.
The sneer when he says "Gringo."

Men dig their own graves.
Yet we too are driven by wants
and feel, even for pathetic thieves
as we hear the executioners' shots

and see the sad hats
being carried by wind
out to that wilderness
where gold mingles with dust.

from 'CITIES'

Travelling, one accepts everything.
-- Elias Canetti *(The Voices of Marrakesh)*

3. FLORENCE

Manly city, once stoical and spare, whose great sculptors
were bachelors. Here, the dialectical eye
moves from mustard, buff, pale yellow, and cream
to the black and white marble of the Baptistery,
the deep green and flashing gold of San Miniato.
Stone worn by time into grandeur is onerous;
it weighs upon the inhabitants who try to fly
on mopeds or in dark Fiats
beneath the bald eyes and open book of their Poet
who consigns them to his newest circle – Sameness.
Transvestites strut outside the American Express Office.
On Ponte Vecchio I haggled for trinkets and thought
of Michelangelo who himself climbed the Tuscan hills
to split stone and load the panting asses.

7. AKKO

Mediterranean city know for conquests and death.
Cannons still face the sea that glints like a scimitar,
that roars with the chilling jubilance of Turkish invaders.
The fortress, calcified with sea-salt and sun,
so white it seems composed of bones.
In a diner, far from my battle of the generations,
I watched two men I imagined were father and son
poised over a game of backgammon
and wondered if distance alters anything.
In a window, a lamb's inverted torso
drew a chorus of fanatic flies,
the room expectant with the sinister
undercurrent of gurgling hookahs,
the punctuated clack of worry beads and dice.

91

8. JERUSALEM

(for Michael and Anita Greenstein)

From Mount of Olives, the gold Dome of the Rock
reflects a sun so intense I can see the blade of Abraham,
hear Mohammed's horse's hooves claw an arid heaven.
In the Arab market, a pyramid of sheep's heads –
the startled congregation. Here the archeologist's job
is permanent for below this city is another,
and below that another as if there were no end to history
which if you succeed in unraveling is God's voice
with its perfect conundrum: "I am who I am,"
sending you back to man. At each station of the cross,
no matter how much banter, you can hear a nail drop.
At the temple wall the pressing intonations out of
the diasporic wind: trials, questions, lamentations.
Beneath my hand the ochre stone turns to skin.

9. HIROSHIMA

In Peace Park Museum, bins of melted
Hirohito glasses, scorched fabric, bone bits,
and the wall of stopped clocks: 8:15.
And 8:15 again. I walked
amongst the unnatural newness
of white buildings, the sun seemed to be burning
through an unclean filter,
the air crackled with the sound of Geiger counters –
I believed I was breathing the contagion of death.
Even the U.S. servicemen were solemn,
eyes fastened to the pavement
where every other block you might stumble on a marker,
a small stone that reads:
School children vanished here.

11. MADRAS

On a scalding pavement, blotches of betel juice
like blood drops trailing from a victim.
Traffic clotted by a procession of elephants.
In this city the head is rearranged by the sun
and the gaping contradictions: a pink palace
rising out of a slum, a white lotus shimmering
in cow dung. Green Bengali sweets in glistening foil
and the vacant eyes of beggars, the dust of wasted soil.
At the old British Fort there are no such opposites
to disorient the traveller: calm-faced generals
and governors gaze out from gilded frames,
their wives shine like porcelain.
And locked in glass cabinets:
log-books, stamps, seals, sabres.

12. AGRA (Taj Mahal)

A rickshaw through Agra's saffron dawn.
Early market: vendors squat and spit.
The smoke of harsh beedees mixes with the fragrance
of cardamom, turmeric. Boys hawk trinkets
on the path to the monument that opposes life's flux:
white marble born out of hurt flesh, grief's darkness,
tomb of a delicate princess, her beauty translated
into latticework and minarets, so dreamlike they seem
to question their existence. They promise to levitate
and join the cumulous jet – eye language.
The rectangular pool before it, cool carpet of water
with its oriental lesson of mirrors
reflecting what is changing, what is changeless.

13. BENARES

Wailing women. A father's body
turns to black diamond then collapses to ash,
sifted into the Ganges with a flurry of white lotus.
The soul is burned to last. Orange garlands,
clasped hands, the third eye, flame-coloured and central.
Naked Saddhus draw water through nostrils,
throat, even rectum, reminding us
that all discipline is a form of purification.
No matter what time of day, time seems frozen:
the heart's standstill, the fluttering will.
A whole city built on a river
for the sole benefit of the soul's departure.
Whoever is brought here is bound to return again.
In the blue flames mourners meet their reflections.

14. BOMBAY

(for Christopher Levenson)

Music and decay. At the Elephanta Caves
great rock sculptures – a who's who
of Hindu deities: Shiva, Vishnu, Garuda, Saraswati.
Chipped faces. Flattened noses and eroded ears.
They resemble the lepers drawing tourists' coins
with their stumps of crusted fingers.
Winged black notes clot the blue Bombay air.
On Malabar I can connect: Hanging Gardens
and Towers of Silence atop which bodies of Parsees
feed birds of prey – a clean vanishing.
Each night a wake for a street kid gone under:
South Indian drums and a quivering, climbing vocal
sends the soul on its looped journey.
Choral darkness. A shower of white petals.

97

MAHABALIPURAM

Rock shrines, stone carvings, south of Madras,
dating back to 600 A.D.

1

The monkey man.
The bare-breasted lovers
riding through air.

A goddess,
coils of the cobra
from the waist down

all caught
in a state of becoming,
their fluidity frozen

they no longer suffer,
acting the warrior, the fool,
the human animal.

In stone
they have been rescued
from the monotonous groan of ocean

and from the interminable cycle
of darkness
and light.

2
In the temple cave
an enormous stone phallus
and a small bas-relief
of the four-armed god, one hand
cupped about his wife's breast.

But we are restless flesh,
not stone. It is always
twilight in the temple.
Through the entranceway
I see the sun-lit beach, blue sea,
brilliant-coloured saris:
the world of energy and waste
which this silence nourishes.

I touch the humid stone
and its coolness opens a space in me
where the darkness collects.
Light sings beyond the cave
and I move to touch it.

SAILOR'S EAR

What had us out those early mornings,
me with pen and paper,
you the boy discoverer combing the shore
for seashells, free treasure?
Smooth spirals, ridged fans.
The tiny ones dropped into a jar of winter sun.
Go ahead, wash and label them.
They have names to look up in a book
like *flamingo tongue, sailor's ear,*
and the three-inch *lettered Venus* –
so much desire in the language you'd think
they'd been invented by anonymous poets,
dreaming seafarers. And my fear
is that our fluid morning hours together
will be reduced to just a photograph
of me in a bleached-out beach chair,
my pen momentarily lifted from the pad,
you in the foreground squinting for the snap
raising your sea-pink trophy
for the instantaneous lens,
the two of us caught in the framed imitation –
so static. What then would I wish?
That in the years to come
when you press this fighting conch
to your ear you hear no duplication,
no dreary note of eternity
but a voice that incites beginnings,
those possibilities that lead to the actual
and what you gathered in your bright pail:
the primal crimsons, cool, crustaceous,
the bivalves' cloud-like swirls of grey,
and their names
sounding our unknowable depths.

PLAYING BASEBALL WITH MY SON

It is more than a sphere of stitched leather
that is passed between the generations
in slow parabola or thrown hard
because a father's love
should sometimes sting the hand.

It takes me back
to weeds in centre field,
the deep lull of a June afternoon
when all things were possible
and I imagined myself to be Mantle.

Icons fed the mythical:
sportscards, record books,
stats of earned-run averages,
lineups of the great
and what they said

all kept in the gum-sweetened darkness
of my boyhood dresser.
I seem to have traded all that
for this mantle of language.
Still, I love the contact:

smack of the ball on leather,
crack of the bat,
drama of an arm outstretched –
the perfectly pocketed
white period

that you hold now,
the tangible confidence
that comes with its weight,
its hardness. It is
a small planet

that you've learned
to make live with curves
and change-ups, those unexpected
shifts that somehow resemble
a life's discontinuous events.

Who knows what fate
will throw us? But this will keep,
burned deep into love's pocket:
the June sun, the diamond,
the white, anchored bases.

HUCKLEBERRY

Aged seven,
I lay in bed with a fever
read to by Mrs. Rowlands, our neighbour,
her voice of seventy years
speaking Huck's green grammar
leading me to the heart's frontier...

My life of longings, escapes.
The continents I've covered,
the million-odd eyes
that have brushed against mine.
Now I know:
that slave I worked to set free
is me – my raft
this tenuous craft
carrying me through currents of darkness
to where the ghosts grieve
because they are misunderstood.
There I see myself,
a runaway boy in the narrow ravine,
walking by the creek
that is forever too shallow,
making my impossible plans.
Attentive to the shrieking birds,
the flying shadows,
I have already entered
into my deep exile
where the trees seem to breathe
and bend
toward a word.

THE PUBLIC PIER

I remember its blond planks
and the initials of lovers
carved with penknife
or burned with a magnifying glass
that had focussed the sun. Hearts,
dates, proclamations of affection
whose endurance no one could guess.
It was held up by a primal crib:
algae-covered timber and boulders
where my feet slipped, where I'd dive
to find blurred bottles, fish hooks,
lost sinkers, lures, and disconnected lines.
Last year I returned to find it gone,
a blue vacancy, a gross and gaping space
that shocked like an amputation,
a confirmation that my friends
doing cannonballs off the edge
to startle the older girls sunbathing
(so mysterious in their dark sunglasses),
anglers, elderly card players, panting dogs,
and ice-cream licking toddlers in strollers
(their young mothers swaying
to static-riddled love songs
from the transistor radios)
were all only sunlit ghosts
breathing in my head.
All things under the sun perish
but under the surface –
broken claws of the crayfish,
the great, moping bass.

SPRAY

Each summer he wonders
if he still has what it takes.
A sudden argument
from the engine and he is yanked
out of the cold cradle of the lake,
his vision blurred
by the wall of white water.
He claims his balance,
adjusts his weight,
cuts hard across the green surface
sending a shiver of spray.
Not as deep or as close
as he did in his youth,
but close enough to know
some vestige of his former self
exists, for there's that shadow
speeding alongside of him,
unaged, dark
and featureless.

THE SUBURBS

I too dislike the scenery:
the uninspired lawns,
the freshly sealed driveways,
the predictable turn of sprinklers.
Those who live with abundance
yet somehow wish for more.

Who can plumb the contradictory depth
of that hunger
and that uneventful ordinariness
that's become an easy target
for both the social worker
and the poet?

For something in us wants this:
a place to be unafraid
and generally unnoticed;
to be quietly productive,
unwilling to admit how prosperity
permits us to live and let live.

It is true. There are painful regrets
and dramas behind each door,
days we would rather forget.
But how considerate the region is
with its regular
goings and comings. Its appearances.

Whatever it is we've surrendered
is sensed in the evening
as we watch the darting birds
cut through thickening dusk
and know that something
larger, something secretive

is held constrained under
the asphalt and pavement. We ask
if there were once gods in the cedars
who have abandoned us. We wonder,
as night wraps around like a mask,
at the pressing disorder of stars.

MAN AND WAVE

So he heard it,
a sibilance rushing the shore,
the drawn-out breathing
of a cosmic sleeper,
lost lullaby heard first in childhood
and before that
the rhythm of maternal blood
echoing through the expectant fluid.
Alien now, he tried to figure what it said.

He walked closer, listening
as if the mystery might be solved
but like suds from a washer
the surf dissolved in the sand
leaving only the bare-chested conundrum
of a man in a swimsuit
freely entering the element
the crest of his self rising
to meet the wave coming in.

LANDSCAPE

In the end, the only country left to
face is the one each has founded:
no hand on the heart, no flag, no anthem.

The sound that a rock makes
when it is rushed at by wind.

THE COLD

In this country
the cold drives people inside.
Their houses swallow them.
The furnace churns
and they sit in the warm belly
of the great house bear,
filled with a private odor.
When they venture out
they wear hats
or ear muffs and resemble
ridiculous animals.
They flap their arms to keep warm
like people-sized birds.

In summer they emerge
but you can see the winter
has not left them. You see it
in their faces, their movements,
in the way they greet one another,
tentatively, as if there may not be
another summer and winter will last and last
like a condition that is chronic.

But they don't walk to the clinic.
They accept it
the way their ancestors once accepted God –
without singing, without celebration

and in August, in the wilderness,
they stare in amazement
at the profusion of green
and accept the naked silence as a hymn.

WINTER FISHING

A hole in the ice in our heated makeshift.
The amber bottle set on a barrel.
And he was pouring it out – I mean tales
one more discreditable than the next

shifting from town rumour to major politics:
histories, grief, the net of self-mocking laughter
while outside the wind sounded out
the miles of lake gone desert.

Against that rawness his voice was a comfort
as we sat blinking over dark punctures,
visualizing the slow torpedo of scales,
the locked eyes in the depths below us

suspended between what is cold and colder.
When he stopped talking the wind came in,
the minutes became hours as nothing took hold
and our lines seemed connected to air.

111

CLUSTERS

Look at the flowers, so faithful to what is earthly,
to whom we lend fate from the very border of fate.
And if they are sad about how they must wither and die,
perhaps it is our vocation to be their regret.

–Rilke

1

What will open and close: doors,
days, eyes, valves, and ventricles.

A canticle then for the impermanent
and what will be repeated.

2

Spring, the predictable and potential.
There was possible blockage:
the brown insulation of leaves,
bleached newspaper trapped all winter,
early weeds. I raked that clear.
Still there were the clods and pebbles
to break through. Seen from the shoots' perspective –
planets, boulders.
But now they're here,
a row of underworld couriers,
your grape hyacinths –
                            delectable clusters.

3

What comes first
should be miraculous.
But I am oddly detached
like the rest of this garden,
still stunned by winter
and by your leaving –
a spectator
of these minuscule bells.

4
Your pale hands planted them,
reaching down into that region
devoid of clouds and angels.
Density of roots, minerals and the strange
meeting of the sixth finger –
thick earthworm, our future worker.

All our years together:
but who are you with your clear eyes?
We were two types: what I saw into,
you saw through. A wind comes up.
There are no leaves yet to rustle.
And your image fluctuates,
is hard to hold onto.

5
And I wonder if it is too late
to define what came between us?
We lived so many years
without drinking these colours,
consumed with concerns, disappointments,
not enough risks ("too many!" you'd say),
not enough tenderness.

I understand your wish to go
once the planting was finished,
but yesterday, while cutting the grass,
I bent to lift a piece of eggshell
on my fingertip,
jagged bit of world,
and wondered if its inhabitant
survived the breakage.

6

The fence has all but vanished.
No one has bothered to raise another
as if neighbours had given up on borders –
a new phase in human evolution.
Why hadn't that seeped into our arguments?
What came between us was a material invisible
yet strict like metal.

Wood chips of posts fifty years old
feed all this struggling green
that will make its appearance
in your absence.

7

Is this then our lives, this
charted lot, this set survey?
Who will talk of the small striving,
fears, watering, the shears I sharpened
("What's cut grows stronger,
but if you cut too much...").
All we can count on are the flowers,
evidence of the kaleidoscopic revolution
from now till autumn,
while we stay the same shade
moving ourselves closer to shades.

8

Was it predictable or strange
that after all those years we still
wondered why the lilac failed to bloom,
whether the juniper was better suited
to the front yard,
asking Mrs. Wilson, our neighbour specialist
for more tips. Her garden, with modest fountain
and butterfly bush, perfect, calm,
though since her husband's death
she's out so seldom.

114

9
His elaborate feeding system:
the birdhouse he built – tubes, funnels.
In winter, I stood amazed at our back window,
watching, one year after his death,
the burning blues and reds flit against snow –
as if they were messengers
from the speechless region.

10
You were good at growing things.
I watched you kneeling with your work-gloves,
trowel, straw hat. You always kept
a quiet distance between yourself
and existence. A form of respect.
I sometimes barge through things,
damaging incipient bulbs
while eradicating weeds.

You taught me care
and now I stand here alone
watching an indecisive bee zigzag
and hover.

11
Perhaps Voltaire was correct –
to cultivate this small tract
is the place to arrive. But then again,
he lived so much in his head.

Still, when you cross an ocean
you're only invading someone else's garden.
Stay, and it becomes your own.

12
And I liked to travel. Once I incited you
to trek across two continents:
temples, sacred rivers, and most persistently –
ruins. My attraction to what is lost, broken,
yours to what is starting up, settling in:
the cup of light, the reflective carpet,
the hand-warmed banister.
While you were arriving, I was leaving,
but now it's you who's taken the major leap.
Perhaps there's a mathematical proposition
to define our states, like lines that won't converge.
Remember leaving Bombay,
and the sharp geometry of train tracks
that consumed the distance?

13
Difficult to know where things end, begin,
and even these words, perhaps an evasion.
But once you said you heard whispering
beneath the level of your deepest digging.
Out of the fragrant darkness,
the hyacinth, with its blood droplets,
ghost breath calling out
from the quietude of your life
to the stirred region, imploring you
to make up for what you had not lived.

14
To dream out of this and go back years
to when I'd write upstairs
looking out the window at the spray of colours
as you filled our daughter's turtle pool.

Her white sun bonnet, small sail
of memory. So long as things were growing,
you were content. Now it's as if
the goddess of fresh starts
had left this garden still growing
but barren.

15
The children encouraged us to plant
what we never thought of: pumpkins,
sunflowers, fiddleheads –
exotic green harps you said you'd play.
Now they're grown and gone
but the space they left –
a no-man's-land across which our words
sputtered like flares
lighting up the injured.

16
And was it "things" that came between us?
Not grief but the scorecard of grievances:
workload, balances, another love interest,
or those vestiges of parents we thought
we'd talked to rocky death,
or perhaps just tedium – no longer in awe
of our own blooming selves.

Uncontrollable forces
like heat waves, dry wind,
sudden hail – unaccountable.
My terrible ego.

17
"A little bit at a time," Mr. Wilson would say,
and his wife would nod.
They never seemed to exert themselves,
yet not a weed. Even the peas
perfectly creeping up their posted screen.

117

Strange though, he died on a journey,
the retired homebody out at sea at 84.
Where was the cruise ship?
Far south of the equator.
Perhaps the air was too strange,
the light unfamiliar?

18
You gone too, but not like that,
not food for the roots of your hyacinths,
just breathing different air, greeting
different neighbours – an elemental difference.
Sometimes, I swear I feel your fingers
in the crusted fingers of your work-gloves.

19
The bearded gardener you liked to joke with
who sells manure and fiery petunias
at the Fairlawn Market, asked after you.
I said you had other things to do.
Was I deceiving him, or me?

20
And life, which once seemed so vast,
is small like this garden,
like the white ribbon on your straw hat
I discovered in the basement cedar chest.
Straw's no conductor
but its strands carried me back through our years.
I sat a long time after finding it,
the silence in that underground room, enormous.

21
All of this, a backward glance.
Have I lost you then, to the darkness of separation?
Those gnawing beasts – regret and self-accusation –
(not having said enough, or too much)
calmed for a time by language.

At night they start up
with narrowing eyes
as if deaf to the songs tossed down
to quell their hunger.

In an engraving
one might see them stupefied
with poetry, peering from behind
the trees of an earlier century.

22
It is summer and the purple of your hyacinths
has evaporated.
Small stalks,
spiky, unspectacular.

23
Our moments are ours.
Flowers return here or to some other garden
with the tedium of the eternal
but what was said between us,
distinct, particular,
binds us to passing flesh.
Tell me, where you are,
is there the smell of darkness,
thick clots of rain soaked loam,
the dense congregation of flowers
drugging the summer air?

24
And things feel incomplete.
It is like a late conversation
broken off in mid-sentence
while some winged thing insists
against the midnight screen.

I keep expecting you to call to me
from our kitchen window but when I turn
there is only the shade of the tree,
a vacant picnic table, July's
heartless doldrums. And now
we have all this finishing to begin.